CO-ARP-813

THE
SEVEN DEADLY SINS
AND OTHER POEMS

THE SEVEN DEADLY SINS

AND OTHER POEMS

DAVID R. SLAVITT

LOUISIANA STATE UNIVERSITY PRESS   BATON ROUGE

Published by Louisiana State University Press
Manufactured in the United States of America
First printing

Designer: Barbara Neely Bourgoyne
Typeface: Whitman, text; Gotham, display
Printer and binder: Thomson-Shore, Inc.

Library of Congress Cataloging-in-Publication Data
Slavitt, David R., 1935–
   The seven deadly sins and other poems / David R. Slavitt.
      p. cm.
   ISBN 978-0-8071-3402-3 (alk. paper)—ISBN 978-0-8071-3403-0 (pbk. : alk. paper)
   I. Title.
   PS3569.L3S48 2009
   811'.54—dc22

                                                            2008026611

"The Phoenix," "The Hermit and the Mouse," "The Six Elegies of Sulpicia,"
and "Après les vents, après le triste orage" appeared in a chapbook, The
Phoenix and Other Translations, published by the New American Press in
2004. "The Seven Deadly Sins" was first published in the Sewanee Review
116, no. 3, Summer 2008. Copyright © 2008 by David R. Slavitt. Some of
the poems have appeared in Per Contra, The Cincinnati Review, The Courtland
Review, Natural Bridge, and Light. The author is grateful to these editors.

for Janet

CONTENTS

TRANSLATIONS

THE
SEVEN DEADLY SINS
AND OTHER POEMS

SLEEP SET: A SONNET SEQUENCE

1 SLEEP SET

After the minutes you've set it for are up,
the radio doesn't just switch off but dwindles,
a gentle diminuendo so that you're never
quite sure when it stopped. Indeed, you continue
to imagine hearing music, or to imagine
music. Come to think of it, light, too,
does something like that, when you've switched off the lamp
and the optic nerve still imagines or, say,

tries to supply on the eyelids' inner surface
patterns of intermittence in the dark
that you cannot swear are not there. Think of the other,
opposite condition, that instant of pregnant
blackness after the Lord had spoken his first
words, when the blinding light was about to be born.

2 SILENCE

Consider Svevo's Zeno, giving up smoking,
or Kafka's hunger artist's more startling feats
of abjuration, or any meditating
Mitzi or Mindy, concentrating on breathing
and trying, minute by exquisitely protracted
minute, not to move a muscle, and you
have arrived at the problem of silence with its discomforts
but its blandishments, too. As the days go by, I discover

how little difference it makes, or ever made,
and I recognize how little anyone cares.
I am not so different or special. Or interesting.
A humiliation of course, but a burden lifting,
or suppose that a fever has broken and, weak as a baby,
and mute, I confront the errors of my life.

3 MOTIONLESSNESS

You're unable to sleep: one tactic is not
to move, to entrance the body and through it the mind
to contrive a repose in oblivion's arms, but the muscles,
nerves, and joints conspire, asserting their will.
The bones, more modest, consent or recognize
their kinship with sticks and stones out there in the darkness,
or do they anticipate that longer stillness
in deeper darkness, when, freed of the flighty meat,

they emerge at last to declare their architecture's
splendor and join their assembled elders, rapt
in their congregation's endless prayers of praise?
I am surprised at that thought and shift yet again,
and scratch an itch, and my bladder mocks, and my gut
comments rudely. But why look to them for wisdom?

4 SILENCE, PROTRACTED

Thicker, richer, almost tangible, silence
in Beethoven's ears was different from yours or mine,
with changes of atmosphere, heavier sometimes,
or lighter, with its slow modulations he learned
to appreciate. Music, one can compose,
but silence, less yielding and shy, demands a submissive
attention, more refined, to apprehend
an import. There is ocean's roar, but under

the ocean, at its heart, a sostenuto
rest, or the moment before the music begins,
with the baton raised, all eyes and ears fixed
on its sharp, quivering point. An angel passes,
but on occasion may pause, decide to sit,
stay, settle, befriend and even bless.

5 TENSE

On the knife edge of past and future, the line of the present
reveals what any tenderfoot can see
is a dull blade that reflects the light, and a whetstone
is what you need. At night, it is harder to tell
except by touch and the risk of drawing blood.
But the knife twists and the flat of the blade, a trowel,
spreads blackness in an action painter's frenzy,
and tenses blur: heaven is time stopping,

but hell is just the same, except you're unhappy,
and instead of rejoicing on ironed sheets, in fear
and torment you toss, turn, and writhe forever.
From how many jumbled nightmares have you struggled
to escape awake into a world that's worse?
And where is that whetted knife when you need it most?

6 TOUCH

Two bodies, in their independent, eccentric,
almost sidereal motions, prompted by stiffness,
pains or itches, or random restlessness,
separate, touch again, and a palm, mine,
on your flank reenacts our courtship and enduring
marriage. Messages sent along the nerves
blur delight to a gentler pleasure and settle
the subtle refinements of touch to simple sensation,

awareness of pressure, the weight of my hand and arm
in an ongoing encounter with your warm
and solid flesh, event transforming itself
to constant condition, the hand on the verge of melting
into your otherness, dreaming of bridging the huge
gap: the marriage, at last and for good, embodied.

7 CASTAWAY

When that tree in the forest falls, the chipmunk hears it,
the ears of the deer perk, and antiphonal chatter
of birds gives way and then recovers, resumes.
More interesting is that brief interval,

the interruption . . .
                        But let us change the scene
to an isolated atoll where gentle surf
sighs and, from time to time, sea breezes blow.
A castaway, exhausted, crawls from the water,

and the silence changes, intensified, aware,
as it was not a moment before, of sentences looming
like clouds high overhead in a parched landscape
in ozoned air where the sky may open up
in a torrent of words—of philosophical discourse,
poems, prayers, or instructions, or insults and lies.

8 MONSTERS

The murk is the brain's brash laziness: asleep,
it cannot be troubled to specify too much,
and, besides, all it wants is results, the emotion, fear
the great vague shape can produce. A sea-cow? A whale?
A shark? But give it a huge eye, one detail
that swims by into clarity from which
to extrapolate to the menace, the helplessness
the dream is about. (But my ready understanding

does not help, cannot keep the monsters at bay.)
The brain, then, mocks itself? But that is its habit,
and I am merely the witness, or am I the arena
where blood—mine—spills every night in this struggle
from which the only escape is to consciousness
where I suffered the wounds these circuses cannot heal?

9 MARINE FORECAST

Not the one I wallow through in dreams
where dimly perceived monsters threaten but cannot
do me harm, this is the real, the only
ocean there is, too wild, too wide and deep
for anyone to know. Respect, they call it,
those who venture out. It sounds far better
than the fear men hate admitting to one another.
They've seen what it can do in its passing moods,

and yet go out, their pennants flapping smartly
in a gentle breeze that does not at all beguile,
and the brightwork all but blinding of confident youth
whose faces are not yet set into bravery's mask,
as if there were no shoals, no sunken hulks,
nor sharks that swim through the murk of my turbulent nights.

10 BEYOND DESCRIPTION

Beyond Description? But who in hell would name
a town "Description"? Somebody who lived there
in the emptiness and the blazing sun where the vein
comes close in the cut in the earth the arroyo made.
By day, it's the Rauschenberg painting, that white canvas
in San Francisco; at night it's the answering work
of Claude Tousignant in Montreal, all black
(*Thanatos* is the pleonastic subtitle).

Out there, the smart and the stupid reunite
in necessity's brotherhood of extremes where any
life at all is assertion and subtlety shrivels
and dies of thirst or freezes and nobody needs
or dares to say, "It's hot," or "It's cold." He rejected
"Despair," sure we'd discover that for ourselves.

11 NAP

It is often sudden, that lovely languor that beckons
and then insists, as the page you are reading dims
and the meanings of printed words shimmer and fade.
You fight it, at least for a while, because who is the master,
you or your body (a stupid question you'd answer
if you were not now so tired)? You lower the book,
or rather watch as your hands let it fall to your chest,
and you dream the next sentence or paragraph

the writer might have preferred. In the late afternoon
it happens often enough: you are unafraid
and have learned to enjoy this heaviness, the falling,
the unsought visit of that god you pray for
so fervently at night. Harmony, grace,
and health, unearned, unlooked for, happy, happen.

12 CAUCHEMAR

From what was I fleeing? Surfacing into the blackness,
I cannot remember what creatures lurked in the depths
of my uneasy sleep, their enormous shape,
their unspecified but terrible threat, or deduce
from their wake in my mind what they were like. But fear
still floats in the dark I recognize as my room,
though it may, in time, diminish. It always has.
With courage, or desperation, I might confront

and fight these beasts, but how can I think such a thing,
knowing that they are mine, are me? My eyes
adjust, the irises widen: the bulk of the dresser
reassumes its usual place and function, no longer
the coffin someone had thoughtfully provided
standing against the wall, convenient and close.

13 WALLPAPER

The dawn does not break so much as it oozes through
not only the window's louvers but even my closed
eyelids enough to register on the cones
and rods of the retina first and then on the groggy
mind some random signals of darkness and light,
the effects of the tissue's vessels the mind interprets
(as it always interprets, looking for patterns and meanings),
and I am persuaded, at least for the moment, that somehow

someone has put up wallpaper inside my eyelids,
a deep, dullish red with random striations and brighter
accents, not unattractive, but what do I do
when I tire of this? What doctor or decorator
repapers eyelids? And then I'm awake, and it's gone:
as the mind, abashed, revises, I rub my eyes.

14 WAKING

That matter can move, that meat can think and speak
I always assumed, but the small child's wonder slept,
snuggled down for decades, the best gift kept
for last, so that now, in the mornings, as I wake,

I marvel as I should have done long ago,
that yet again I can gather my spirits to stir
heavy protesting flesh that would much prefer
inertia and flirts with entropy. I know

that each day's triumph, however unlikely, is cause
in a losing war for modest celebration,
but defeat is at least postponed by each battle won:
I heave myself up to a sitting position, pause
a moment, and am amazed by what I have done,
having reenacted the miracle of creation.

CANDLE

The candle stays in the closet. Who has the heart?
I cannot recite the prayer I know how to say,
or say I have learned how not to say it. The wick

is white and the candle would burn with a yellow and white
light, but in my heart, the flame, though hot,
is black, black as the dark it would burn in, blacker

than blind men imagine: think of those holes in the sky
that have turned away in disgust, or rage, or despair
from what can be done under what we still call heaven.

TABERNACLE

It was too easy when God was everywhere
to give his comfort and hearken to our prayer,
and too familiar: we took his presence for granted.
Loving us so, but this was not what he wanted
and so withdrew to his tabernacle, rich
with the gold and precious stones he had specified—
but this impoverished the rest of the world in which
his absence prompted us now to look inside.

Did he demand those jewels to provoke desire,
intensify and focus our wanting ardor
with this pasha's display? Or do we dare to put
the question another way, tougher and harder—
was he mocking us with the diamonds' and rubies' fire,
less precious than what had been everywhere underfoot?

CRITIC

The cat torments the toy mouse, shakes and flings it,
chases it, stalks and pounces, knowing full well
it is no real mouse but is satisfied with the rough
similitude, or call it the metaphor—

except that she does not publish or fret about readers
and would never undertake to teach her games.
But any day a critic may appear
to evaluate her practice and test her wit.

Then metaphor will break down; she'll rip him apart
and leave his head on the rug like a ghastly rosebud.

REMINDER

We behold their periodic hyperabundance,
hear it, and fear it . . . the sky thick with locusts,
so many that even the birds' voracity
is utterly inadequate. They eat
maybe fifteen percent. The rest forage,
reproduce, die, and fall to the ground to surfeit
the hunger of rodents and then decompose to enrich
the soil with their burst of nitrogen: the duff

is suddenly what only tender greenhouse plants
ever experience, cosseted, fertilized.
All that ravening, all that copulation
ends up there, in a nutrient flush on the woodland
floor where bellflowers, once every seventeen years,
bloom as they did when they first flourished in Eden.

THE DOGFISH

It isn't true, but Aelian's account
of the Dogfish sets one wondering—can their young,
swimming alongside the mother and taking fright,
return to the womb until the danger has passed
and it's safe to be born again? Probably not.
Some dogfish are viviparous, but their pups
do not behave as Aelian says although who,
at moments of panic, would not accept such a rain check

and choose to recommence life at a better time?
But during that second gestation, do they return
to a fetal tranquility we can no longer imagine,
or do they remember that first fearsome foray?
The wails of our reluctant newborns are dreadful,
but for these, who are born again, how much worse must it be?

BEAST

It's always a man, or so the children suppose,
who've been warned about men and fear them (even boys
learn thus to fear themselves), but the world is different
and mostly worse, and these children's stories turn
ugly and more sordid than we'd expected.
Fiddle a bit with the genders to demonstrate
our sophistication and liberal politics:
let the Beast this time be some old woman,
widowed, probably more than once, and rich
as any of those old moneybags she'd married.
Let Beauty be the boytoy she has picked up
at the spa, plage, ski slope, or boîte she likes,
and our sympathies, confused, skitter and flee.
The young man, lazy and vain, is driven by greed
or need more than by lust, and we are distressed.
Outrageous! Has he no pride, no self-respect?
Yes, too much to work as a shipping clerk
or salesman—he is smart enough but lazy
and has always had it easy, his good looks
having paved whatever way he happened to choose.
Anyway this is not a career but a lark,
a temporary accommodation the suits,
watches, rings, and cuff links have made attractive.
It's almost a joke, but which of them is the butt?

Time passes, and he grows restless, even resentful
and bridles at their imbalance, which he corrects
at first with mere inattention but then, more drastic,
infidelities—pick-ups in bars, or once,
in Cannes, some old guy's pretty young companion,
semblable, soeur. The countess, of course, finds out,
and would throw him out on the spot but he's such a beauty . . .
Or is it rather that she is shrewd and knows
what he is and what he is worth? She doesn't
for whatever reason fuss, and for that he is grateful,

and she is amused. They become, in a way, friends
and stay together all winter, longer than either
could have expected—
                              for Beast understood all along
that beauty is fragile, ephemeral, and sad,
and even in children's stories, Beast wins in the end.

FOG

That dense fog I'd been groping through, cursing
at every tentative step I took, lifted
at least for an instant so that I could glimpse
on every side the dangerous chasms, worse

than anything I had imagined. Then, at some slight
shift in the wind, it closed in again, thick
as ever and leaving me worse off than before.
It was no dream but the waking truth of aging,

common to everyone, the depressing secret
nobody tells us, not even our parents—
out of kindness, perhaps, for they know that sooner or later
we each come to this place and learn for ourselves.

STUPID

The sneezing having abated, the throat no longer
sore, I am nonetheless less, exhausted, stupid
as if my mental rheostat were turned down.
Paragraphs in books became opaque.
Even the talk on the radio faded in
and out, its reception fine but mine not.
An interesting adventure, one might have imagined,
but stupidity finds nothing interesting,

infecting, dulling the whole world down to itself,
with the one brilliant, heartbreaking exception—
that the dreams of the stupid are vivid as yours or mine,
their colors as bright, their mysteries all the more
mysterious and profound. Beyond, beneath
that intelligence we hold dear, they come into their own.

WHAT IS POETRY ABOUT?

Or ask, rather, what earthly good is it,
when a trivial thing like not being able to find
my silver and amber pillbox can ruin my morning?
It's somewhere here, I had it yesterday, I couldn't have lost it,
but I can't find it, which is as good as or as bad as.
One ought not to be too attached to objects, of course, and it is uneconomic
to pay a psychiatrist more to hear one's kvetches about losing, say, a pillbox,
than the thing cost in the first place. But then think of the vessels
at Balthazar's feast, not just cathected objects,
but holy, stolen out of the Temple by his father, Nebuchadnezzar.
This pillbox was from Krakow, a gift from my daughter.
We'd had a lovely day at Auschwitz . . . No, seriously, a good day,
with a Purim service at the end of it, and the old men, the remnants, the relicts,
chanting about Haman and his ignominious end in Shushan.
If you're going to Auschwitz, you should go *erev* Purim,
which makes it bearable. And the pillbox was a memento of that.
So I dug through pockets of trousers and jackets, looked in the nightstand drawer,
peered under the bed, in a trivial but desperate
tizzy. Not to drag it out too exquisitely,
it was on the floor beside the nightstand, where the cats had knocked it
or left it after having played a little pillbox hockey,
which is as good as pinecone hockey with what they can snatch
from the guest bathroom potpourri. And everything was better,
I had it in hand and could relax, or at least stop worrying about that.
I've given up looking for the pen one cat or the other knocked off my desk,
not an important pen, but one I liked,
but I have forgiven them because what is the point in not forgiving them?
And they are dear cats, now that I've figured out
how their licking each other and then fighting, and then running around like
   dervishes
reminds me of my mother and my Aunt Vera, because these two
are also sisters and have a sororal connection, not
altogether pacific but deeply attached. So I forgive them for this, too,
which is easier, now that I have the pillbox back in my pocket.
Nebuchadnezzar was punished for having taken the vessels from the Temple,

went mad, and, like a beast, ate grass. Or if he wasn't punished,
he just happened to go mad, which was, to the Jews who observed it,
significant. More modern ones might simply suggest that he see a shrink
and talk about whatever was bothering him, so that even if he was still unhappy
he would at least stop grazing like a bull in a meadow.
It's the grass at Auschwitz that is misleading.
A friend of mine who was there, who was really there,
told me that they ate all the grass, not crazy but just hungry.
And poetry? Is what holds all this together, what keeps me
more or less together, or at least is a way of changing the subject.

HOME

To throw the black stones as we walk away, to say
we will never return to this hateful place, to spit,
to shit in stone on this vile place where the vile .
thing happened is easy: it will not stay,
but follows, a mangy cur, a distressed cat
that in desperation overcomes fear to beg
from us some scrap or merely a kind word.
Years later, and many, many miles away,

that horrible place slinks back, a step at a time,
in dreams: a house, the look of a street, the familiar
sky, innocent once, under which we,
innocent, played as if there were no taint waiting.
And when I die and am taken back there, my children
shall leave on my grave black stones to mark their visits.

PRAYERS

Now and again in the incomprehensible spate
of words they are droning or singing, sitting or standing,
some phrase floats by that connects, that I recognize
and that tantalizes, if it does not enlighten.
A child picks out in some such manner, pattern,
matter, meaning, but I have forgotten almost
all I ever knew of the tongue of prayer
and learning, and am ashamed at my lack, and, wordless,

pray that my innocence, ignorance's twin,
will save me, and my yearning intelligent men
around me cannot feel. Will the Lord reach out
with a mother's beckoning arms to invite and encourage
the unsteady steps I take to travel across
what turns out to be, after all, a little space?

GLIMPSE

The menacing serpent that turns, upon closer inspection,
into a glimpse through the bushes of garden hose
continues nevertheless to arouse . . . not fear
anymore but its echo, a keener awareness of danger
that lurks not there where we thought but just out of sight
and that we've avoided if only by blind luck
we understand we cannot trust. A near
miss is perhaps instructive; the hit would be deadly.

In the parallel universes that physicists posit,
both things can happen at once, the snake and the hose,
in which case these misprisions are chinks in the wall
of the world, are intimations of otherness, true
if not here then somewhere as, somewhere else,
those bushes we saw are burning and are not consumed.

HIGH-SCHOOL PLAY

"A Midsummer's Nightmare" is what the play can turn into
on high-school stages where the young actors' reach
exceeds their grasp and they shriek and still can't be heard:
Helena, in a touch of directorial
madness, enters munching brownies to show
adolescent grief, and with her mouth full mangles
the lines to a Polish translation, but . . .Why not?
The play ends, after all, with those rustic mechanics'

absurd production, the play-within-a-play
that is bad by intention but shows us Pyramus dead
and Thisbe, too, as Shakespeare reminds us how love
is no laughing matter, the neat pairing off to follow
a contrivance that could have gone wrong, and that tragedy lurks
in the wings—and even the hearts of these talentless children.

FIFTIETH-REUNION POEM

June 2006

What it can claim beyond the mere sentimental
attachment it ought to have taught us not to give in to
uncritically is a muddied set of ideals
about which it cannot afford to be too specific:
elitist and yet inclusive, maintaining the old
traditions but welcoming others (almost any),
and that sense we share of owning and belonging.
Nevertheless, it's Yale, and if it is not
ours, we are still its, beat up and taking
pills, but happy to be here with one another.
(Those who came are happy; I pray for the others,
who couldn't or wouldn't, our brothers, uncomfortable here
fifty-odd years ago or, for whatever reason,
now, wherever they are: forgive us, forgive
yourselves!)
                        What we know, we mostly learned later.
Here, what we studied was how to learn and how
to get on (at least as useful, if somewhat vulgar).
Like-mindedness (whatever it was Yale looked for,
we were the ones it chose, and we were and mostly
still are not unalike) is an undervalued
comfort, rare and, as we get older, more
than ever convenient. They would not choose us now.
We were Eisenhower's students as much as Griswold's—
his interstate system, badly in need of repair,
couldn't, like our class, be built today.
The competition, they say, is keener now,
but are present students better, or merely and oddly
different, or, say, more diverse? Now, there are women—
students and faculty, too—and that's a good thing,
but not without its costs: fifty years ago
Yale was clubbier, even a bit stupid,
but young men on their own can be pleasingly coltish.
Women of that age are already grown-ups,

and, as we have learned, there is plenty of time for that.
The administration doesn't like to shine
excessive lux on the veritas: fund-raising
is what keeps us connected now, although they are rich,
richer than any of us, and a center of power
of the kind we learned here to suspect. Were these merely
charming illusions, or more than that, legitimate
expectations of how men should treat one another?
An economist runs the place (as at Harvard, too),
and because they are convinced that what they are doing
is wonderful, and New Haven is depressed,
they are thuggish now with even more thuggish unions.
Face it: our Yale is gone, as my father's was
when my son and daughter studied here. His classmate,
Rudy Vallee, sang, "My time is your time."
We'd like to believe it but we know better. Cole
Porter, who still is Yale's preeminent poet,
was closer to the truth—that "it was great
fun, but it was just one of those things."

    Traces of difference persist. Harvard was serious;
Princeton was just a bit louche; but Yale was dapper,
urbane, as even our grandchildren recognize,
and still that's something to which they can aspire.
It may be that aspiration itself is the heart
that keeps the old blue blood circulating, a sense
of high purpose, vague, but not for that reason
contemptible. Taste, cultivation, learning
are never secure but here still enjoy lip service,
and from time to time, at night, in some lighted window
you can see from a quad looking up, in that room that was once
ours many years ago, that something goes on
that God and country need, now more than ever.

LIVE CASTING

A frog in bronze, or a bronze crab with its raised
claws that can, on a desktop, hold quill pens,
both of them done in demoniac detail,
are arresting—but then, they were arrested, the sculptors'
trick being not to create but merely translate
from nature's domain to art's in these live castings,
a modest if murderous exercise by which
they outlast the artists' patrons, the artists,

and us, who gaze at them and whom they defy,
knowing how our admiration can turn
in time to envy of what is immortal. What life-like
pieces around them aspire to, these remember
with longing and bitterness dimming slowly together.

VISITING HOURS

To visit the dying can be a refinement, the dreck
of daily living having receded to leave
only serious stuff, and you're ill-prepared,
self-conscious, and all but tongue-tied. But this is the truth
of your lives, of both your lives, that the awkward encounter
has clarified for you. Or reduced you to.

You don't want to stay too long—not to tire him out,
or yourself, for that matter. And after you've left, you feel
bad, if less bad than he, but for both your sakes,
and wishing it had gone better. And he must have had
such wishes, too, more general, though, and more fervent.
But that's what life is, and you fumble through it.
You do what you can, accepting the limitations:
clumsy, brief, almost dumb, but you were there.

HERALD

Anthemocritus' death? Who can remember
such arcane details? He was sent as a herald
to explain to the Spartans what Athens' embargo meant
and reassure Sparta that closing their ports to Megara's
ships and goods did not have to mean war.
He was, anyway, killed, perhaps by Megarians,

or maybe by Spartan agents: war—and the end
of Greece—followed. The trigger? The tipping point?
Athens' Archduke Ferdinand, unimportant,
except that you never know. Empires shudder
and fall, and any yutz can be the occasion.
He couldn't have known but might have taken comfort
from the general wreck of Pericles and Athens,
of Sparta, Megara, everything, everyone.

RUMINATING

is not the same as thinking, goes nowhere:
I think I am thinking as I chew on the same cud
of fears and regrets, but it's my soul I gnaw,
while time has gagged, so that the past and future
choke together as the bleak field expands
to include whatever the eye of God would see
if it dared look. What I pray for is not this.
And if this is the truth, I want to turn away.

Ask what that cow has to look forward to,
what thoughts she might have but of ruin and the sweet
calves she barely remembers, taken away
so soon that they have blurred together and bawl
and she can hear their piteous voices echo
in the still air and terrible sunshine shimmer.

AZRAEL

Surely, he must exist. How else explain
the shudder we feel from his shadow and fluttering wings?
He has many names, Sammael, Metatron,
Adriel, Abaddon . . . Sometimes Gabriel
performs the office. But Azrael, let us call him—
the help of the Lord—and let us suppose he carries
the envenomed sword of legend with which he dispatches
victims. Was poisoned steel the very worst

they could imagine? Or was there a kindness in it
akin to that of mosquitoes' injected fluid,
a gentling neurotoxin, anesthetic,
so that the merest prick we're not sure we feel
is enough to enlist the body and free the soul,
the decision having already been made elsewhere?

FANTASIA FOR SOLO TROMBONE

The trombone
rarely performs alone.
Albeit loud,
it is almost always part of a large crowd.

But that does not mean
it is lacking at all in spirit, for by a keen
and subtle transposition in the head
of the trombonist, all scores may be reread

as concerti for trombone—in which
the other parts recede into a rich
but deferential background to the clear
voice of the instrument that fills his ear.

And then, at home,
in the cork-lined practice room with the metronome,
where he goes over and over again the great
glissandi and counts the beats of the long wait

until he comes in again,
he is a soloist, most fortunate of men,
who finds in the composer's odd
arrangement of notes a hint of the music God

must like in heaven where angels in their choir
do not so much sing as imagine together a higher
harmony in which all ears and hearts
in simultaneous solos play their parts.

NU, A SESTINA

"According to Sol [Steinmetz], one of the world's great lexicographers . . .
a data-bank search shows *klutz* to be among the Top 10 Yiddishisms in English.
The others: *glitsch, kosher, bagel, maven, mensch, schlock, schmooze, tush,* and
chutzpah."

      —WILLIAM SAFIRE, On Language, *New York Times,* August 28, 2005

With a half a dozen words, you think you can schmooze
in Yiddish? You think that makes you some kind of maven,
to hold forth to one and all with maybe a bagel
(blueberry? chocolate?) in your hand, a mensch?
Face it, what you are is a pain in the tush,
light in the knowledge department but heavy on chutzpah.

Not that that's irrelevant. Some chutzpah
is useful now and then. To be a mensch
you can't just wait around, sit on your tush,
and expect the world to bring you a toasted bagel
with your morning coffee. You have to learn to schmooze
with the right people, and find yourself some maven

to learn the ropes from. You may not be a maven,
or at least not right away, but if your tush
has any sitzfleish, and if you are a mensch,
you'll pick up some of the basics, learn to schmooze,
and, less and less relying on sheer chutzpah,
you'll know which is the lox and which is the bagel,

and maybe even learn that, beyond the bagel,
there are bialys and salt sticks that a deli maven
might prefer. But a goy would need some chutzpah
to order one of those to show he's a mensch
who can fit in well with anybody and schmooze,
a guy who, in the dark, can find his tush.

A silly exercise? You say, "Pish tush!"
But who are you? And where do you get your chutzpah?
A few Yiddish words, and you think with your toasted bagel
with Lite cream cheese you become right away a maven
of the griefs of the Jews, entitled now to schmooze
with rabbis and scholars, a kenner now, a mensch?

It isn't so easy, boychick, to be a mensch.
It requires patience and faith as well as chutzpah.
For suffering, there isn't any maven
from whom you can pick up tips. A kick in the tush
is what you'll learn from. That, and a toasted bagel
will get you a place at the table to sit and schmooze:

Oy veh! A naarishkeit! A mensch? A maven?
A chutzpadickeh gonif! A pain in the tush!
Thus will you learn to schmooze. Another bagel?

THE PUSSYCAT POEM

I love little Pussy,
His coat is so warm,
And if I don't hurt him
He'll do me no harm.
We'll sit by the fire
And I'll give him food,
And Pussy will love me
Because I am good.

That it has to be said is sad: the child is expressing
a hope more than reporting how things are.
The cat is one of those tetchy beasts that sometimes
will suffer caresses, but sometimes not and either

stalk off on some mysterious errand or else,
in annoyance, extend its claws, strike with a quick
paw, and even draw blood. This is the fear
that gives the nursery rhyme its power. The dream

at the end is of a bargain and of a nature
that isn't always fair but might, through our fervent
prayer, behave itself at least for a while—
the fervor a function, alas, of unlikeliness.

It is, therefore, a woeful poem, the child
having learned much of what the cat has to teach her
of what to expect in the world—that good intentions
may meet with hurt and betrayal, and even so,
even if Pussy behaves now and then badly,
we must learn somehow to accept it and, if we're able,
and want to avoid doing ourselves worse harm,
we must find it in our hearts to forgive and to love.

A LESSON FROM THE MASTER

"And now the quick sun, / Rounding the gable, / Picks out a chair,
a vase of flowers, / Which had stood till then in shadow."
　　—From "For Dudley"

A graceful Wilbur turn, impressively modest,
it resonates, so that Fitts's life becomes,
in that elegiac trope, that light that picks out
and enlivens common objects to make them mean
whatever they mean, significant if not holy.

But Wilbur's lines are not the same on the page
of the book on your lap, or desk, or the Levenger gizmo
that allows you to read in bed without having to prop
the volume on your knees. To get them right,
you must go to the small graveyard behind the chapel,

the inn, the art gallery, where a few favored
masters are laid to rest on academy grounds,
and there, on his plot, over his interred body
lie down, supine, looking up at the clear
blue Massachusetts sky where that quick sun

rides serenely—you have to do this to see
on the bottom of Dudley's grave marker those words
incised. It isn't stone, but a flat surface
of sculpted metal on a base and angled stand
a few inches high, so that only from ground level

can you see what is written there. And knowing this,
you're invited or even dared to lie down on the duff
that covers his bones and become, at least for a moment,
like him—which is how he lived most of his life,
teaching the youngsters not only how to read

and write, if they had the talent, but how to see
what, until then, had been in shadow, and how
to be. I have not, myself, performed this rite,
too stiff in the joints and old enough now not to need
such a memento mori, but I am pleased

to imagine students doing this, on a dare,
or to join the club, or however it happens. They learn
more on that turf, I'd expect, than in most classes
from a master who, by this macabre maneuver,
has claimed by embodying those graceful lines.

A CONSOLATION FOR RIGOLETTO

At the end, Rigoletto weeps for his daughter who sings
of rejoining her mother in heaven and la la la . . .

But wake up, clown, think, and reconsider
the action. At least read the damned libretto:
she disobeyed you (well?); and she was a slut,
going off that way at the first chance to fuck
the duke (well, even so?); but worst of all
she was a melodramatic fool, which is not
what the world permits, or sensible fathers, either.

If Sparafucile hadn't killed her, you
would have been right to do the job yourself.

RIO MAR

All day the black *changos* dart over the poolside
chaises, grabbing Tostito crumbs and sounding
a call like a cop's whistle. Later, at night,
the little coquis, those free-toed, almost transparent
frogs reply in repeated microwave beeps
as if Puerto Rico's entire population
were crooks and short-orders cooks. As if! As if!

EASTER ISLAND HEADS

The charm of those huge heads on Easter Island
is in how they diminish day by day as the wind
scours them smooth, abrading away detail
that individuates. We admire their slow

retreat to some Platonic idea of themselves
in which they can meet and merge, as we hope ourselves
to do in some versions of heaven. Our faces, meanwhile,
fall away from that Greek ideal, sag, wrinkle

into increasing crackelure, or, worse,
cruel parody. Also our minds erode
and we lose proper nouns, events, and all those stupid
details to a steady, purifying sea wind.

AVE VERUM CORPUS

Indistinct through the steamed glass of the shower
where the sluice of hot water washes away
irrelevant details as in an abstract
painter's version, I can see the pink
female blur of your body, not merely a happy
vision but the vision of happiness
that painter would have had in mind. No mind,
no idea, but flesh dissolving, contented,

scented of course with some floral soap, and turning
as a comfortable cat will turn, lolling, as if
it can't contain in its small compass so much
delight—not in itself, but, unselfconscious,
unselfish—in its being. And your being,
eyes closed, the water streaming down, I love.

IN MEMORY OF MY UNCLE

He died, an infant, before my mother was born
or I had even been imagined, but still
by right he is or would have been my uncle.
Smaller, less solid than those I knew, this uncle—
or let us call him avunculus—is a tiny,
friendly creature, putto-like. I think of him
looking down from the painting's upper edge
to wish my mother well, and, if his angle
through fluffy Tintoretto clouds permitted,
also glancing sometimes at me. By now,
he is surely resigned to the brevity of his life.
Small children then, before antibiotics,
were death's familiars, and parents had to be tougher
or somehow learn to bear it. But for the children's
ghosts it could have taken a while to see
what they'd been spared and how the bargain wasn't
quite so bad. Only then could they care
for that brother or sister who followed and for whom
their parents' love was more intense, refined
by that grief from which they never quite recovered.
One of my mother's names was Chaya—life,
that my grandparents now knew was fragile and precious.
My uncle? Would he have been amused? Indulgent?
Pleased perhaps to have been memorialized?
We think of our dead as wise, even dead children,
which makes them close but strange. *Mein kleine feter,*
now that my other aunts and uncles have joined you,
and my parents, too, are you the eldest who sits
at the head of the table? Do they serve you first
and defer to your opinions? Not that they need
your wisdom, but rather your lucky purity—
you never told a lie—and you returned
an altogether unsullied soul, which earns you
respect and if not envy, then call it yearning.

I sometimes imagine our meeting, sooner rather
than later, and how I shall take my place at the foot
of that long dining-room table where he presides.
I shall remain uncharacteristically silent
for what may seem like and may indeed be years.
But eventually, he will deign to acknowledge my presence
and even invite a question, and I shall ask
why nowhere in the Torah is there mention
of children like him who died, and the crisis of faith
that must have followed in their parents' hearts.
I can almost see his look, a profoundly sad
baby's look, and being an infant he makes
no answer, or not in words, although he allows
as masters often do, that I may try answers:
that the Torah is what to believe, not how to believe;
that there would have been no point in Moses explaining
what everyone already knew or ought to have known;
that this is why we turn to heaven where silence
is also an answer; that this is a childish question,
and if, someday, I ask a better one, maybe
he will then give me an answer that, of course,
I will no longer need. And then, as my father
did when he was old and tired, my uncle
points to the teapot. Asking? Inviting? Both.

HIGHWAY POEMS

In Memory of Aubrey Goodman

A little south of "Historic Waxahachie"
(for what, I'd like to know), you pass, to the west,
Ace Pick a Part, and either you smile or groan,
or else your heart breaks for this junkyard owner
to whom the phrase, low-level poetry,
occurred. His grime-blackened fingers still clutched
the yellow pencil stump as he realized
that you pick a part and then you pick apart
one of his cars to get the piece you need.
Memorable speech, tmesis, really,
but for him, how many times in his life is it likely
to happen? We do this, it's our trade, our talent,
but for him? It was magic. Inspired. The sign is huge,
and I'd guess it works. People notice. (The Ace?
It's not his name but a way to lead the list
in the Yellow Pages.) He gets up every morning,
has his breakfast—for all I know a MoonPie
and a Dr. Pepper—and then goes off to work
at the junkyard next to the sign with his line, his life.
Farther south, in West (that's the name of the town),
a couple from Prague have built a motel they called,
after a great deal of time and thought, Czech Inn.
It's everywhere, this impulse. We see these poignant,
poor, but honest efforts, and shake our heads,
but we ought to pay attention to these highway
poems, squeezed hard from the mental murk
with their shimmering words and phrases, and learn to labor
with our own pencil stubs, one line at a time.

ACKNOWLEDGMENT

for G. G., obit 2006

More than fifty years ago,
she survived those selections marching around
naked in that circle on bare ground,
trying to look as though

she were still healthy, useful, still
an able worker. Mengele would pick
those he thought were weakening or sick
and whom now he might as well kill.

In her dreams that grave parade
must have gone on forever, until, at last,
the angel picked her, too, as she went past
sick now and still afraid.

In time, we are all selected,
but for her, as a courtesy, beneath his white
robes, the angel had put on that night
the polished jackboots she expected.

GATOR

Not swimming, not even dangling her feet
into the water, but walking along the shore
as any one of us might have done in the heat
of a Florida afternoon, she took it for

a log. It's their little trick. The other greater
is that, for a short distance, they're very fast.
In terror she ran and ran, but the alligator,
clumsy but strong, was even faster. At last

it caught her in those huge jaws that we fear
still in our reptile brains and dragged her back
to the water and in and under to disappear.
The reports say it was the third gator attack

that month, a confirmation that our first
fears were justified when we ventured down
from the trees to where we always knew the worst
saurians lurked in the water and on the ground

where there was more food and comfort. And they may have hoped
for the betterment for the species, but the laws
of nature are harsh and as our ancestors loped
through the rich savannas, the cost was those gaping jaws.

QUIET, CHILDREN

"Quiet, children, quiet for goodness' sake,"
or if not goodness', then because a cake
was in the oven, and stomping might make it fall,
(or else someone was sick and that trumped all
other concerns.)
        I'm quieter now, and many
friends are sick and dying—but does this do any
good for them? I doubt it, but I take
a little boy's consolation, imagining cake.

A TALE OF LOVE AND DEATH
(OR THE LESSONS OF LITERATURE)

Montaigne mentions a girl
who threw herself from a high
window, preferring to die
than yield herself to that churl

whom fate had billeted there.
When the fall did not end her life,
she cut her throat with a knife,
but survived that, too. O rare

and virtuous maiden! Or so
one might think. But the inquiry found
there had hardly been adequate ground
for such drastic behavior. No,

the soldier never attacked her,
but merely sent verses and flowers,
sang songs, and mooned for hours—
which could only confuse and distract her.

One would think she'd have gone along,
for men in the taverns would say
she was fun and an easy lay.
And that's where the young man went wrong,

letting her know what a treasure
he thought she was and had.
This confused her and made her feel bad
rather than giving her pleasure.

Her whole life till then, she knew,
had been a miscalculation.
Far better than fornication
is having a young man woo,

lovesick, desperate, and cute.
How to respond to such stuff?
To fuck him wasn't enough!
What she could think of to suit

his ardor was thus to behave.
Perhaps he might kill himself, too.
It would be the sweet thing to do.
And he'd carry her face to his grave!

COUGH

In the movies, even one cough
means that by the end that character will be carried off
by consumption or some less specific Krankheit.
The cough, therefore, has become a semiotic
indication, an omen no narcotic
mixture relieves. A real cough the actor might make
would be edited out as if it were some mistake,
and his character's survival would be in spite
of the convention to which we all long ago agreed,
or a bold intrusion into the fiction
by the avant-garde director hoping that we'd
react in shock at this naked depiction
of realismo. What could an audience do
or say? If somebody nearby sneezes, you
say, "God bless you," or "Gesundheit." But for this
we have no response or mode of defense. This is
the real world, maybe a prodrome or maybe not.
And you hope that you don't get what he has got.

SNOWBANKS

Inklings? Or aspirations but they float downward,
and the silent transformation is underway,
the schmutz redeemed, the grit smoothed, as if prayers
could still be answered. We know better, of course,
having seen many snowstorms before and having felt
this same delight—if less and less each time—
as the white robes trees and bushes volunteer
as silent choristers. If it could happen to them,

then maybe to us? But it doesn't stay, nor does it
just go away, but they plow it into piles
that do what we do, lose our good looks with age,
diminish, turn brindle, almost black, and, ugly,
call out to us their encouragement, for they have,
maculate, obstinate, bleeding slowly, held on.

GETTING LATE

A good party, but it gets late
and only a few in the cozy living room dawdle.
Our hostess offers another coffee,
which I should refuse, having seen our host
stifle a yawn. But it's dark outside and I risk
rudeness, I know, in accepting. But I do.
I know I shall have to go in a little while.
Like a child making bargains about bedtime,
I want a few minutes more. Just a few minutes.

THE SEVEN DEADLY SINS

1 PRIDE

Surely, there must be some mistake. I admit
at once that my name is there with the other six,
but after all, if you look at what I am
and what I do, as you should not only for my
sake but your own, and examine in however
perfunctory a fashion before passing
judgment, you will realize that I have about me
a certain dignity, even a moral weight,
and that my contribution over the generations
has been by no means negligible. Only call me
self-respect, or, avoiding false modesty, *honor,*
and where are we then? In what way are my promptings
sinful? Pride gives men a reason for doing
the right thing even when the world
has gone mad. Without any self-regard,
I suggest that a man is helpless, very likely
depressed, and could at any moment go
native. In this light you must concede
that I am one of the bulwarks of decency: I
embody not only ethical norms but also
standards of good taste in dress and deportment
as well as in art and music without which
civilization would long ago have toppled.
A sin? No, I'm a virtue and have my pride.

2 ANGER

This is, to say the very least, annoying,
but as you see, I am calm, I am in control.
I should like to point out, however, that the capacity
for anger is morally neutral, and even, sometimes,
a good thing. Does injustice make you angry?
Do cruelty and suffering not engage
your emotions? Intellectual disapproval

is never enough. What you want is your blood to boil,
to seethe with fury at the outrageousness of what
you cannot tolerate, and mankind ought not to permit.
Anger, or call it instead *righteous wrath,*
is an aspect of the divine, and if we partake
to any degree in that perfection, then we
also feel rage at what goes on around us.
For me to be classed as one of the seven deadly
sins is enough to make anyone angry,
but what's wrong with that, as long as I maintain
proper decorum? The mental state, the mere
idea of anger cannot be sinful. Any
random thought that crosses your mind . . . Are you held
accountable for that? Then you are all
eternally damned—that is if you still believe
in damnation and those scary Italian pictures
of the last judgment with the shrieking souls falling
on one side of the canvas, and, on the other,
beatific wimps ascending, smiling,
full of the gas of gentle piety.
Do you want to be one of those? Do you? I ask you.
Grow up, accept who you are, and accept me.

3 AVARICE

I know what you're about to say: *radix
malorum est cupiditas.* I admit
that, in Latin, it has a nice ring to it, but let us
be frank with one another and try to imagine
a world in which there wasn't at least some degree
of *cupiditas.* The industrial revolution
is erased, the capitalist system in which mankind
is better off, at least in a material way,
than it ever has been since they rooted about
for acorns. Ambition? The desire for betterment,
for one's self and family too, the eagerness
for respect that society shows, it cannot be
denied, in financial terms, the only language

universally understood . . . You want to chuck
all that? What are you, some kind of left-wing dreamer?
Greed can get out of hand (but then what can't?)
and be carried sometimes to grotesque excess.
And if that is the case, then Greed isn't the sin
but Excess—which oddly does not appear on the list.
A roof over your head, a decent bed,
a nice house, or maybe even a little
more than that? A car that's fun to drive
and you're on the road to hell? Does that make sense?
Who's left? You want to go and live on a commune?
Or maybe some simple place in the third world?
Well, maybe you do, but only because it's cheaper,
you can get good servants for next to nothing, and live
remarkably well on what your portfolio yields.

4 ENVY

The rest of them envy me, and I admit
that I am pleased by this. It's always nice
when somebody looks at your ring, your stickpin, your wife,
the emeralds at her neck and on her bosom,
and smiles to hide the grinding of his teeth
as he admits to himself (but you know, too)
that you are the alpha male. The other six
are on the list, but I am the only one
who appears as well in the Ten Commandments, which galls them.
Not that this makes me especially heinous or different,
for who does not feel envy when window-shopping
on Madison in the sixties? He's blind, or dead,
or he has so much, himself, that he only knows
envy from the receiving end, for it
is a two-way street. You crave what this man has,
or how much he knows, or how good he looks, or his youth
or health, or his success, or his children's . . . Of course,
you do, and this is a goad to work harder.
Take a longer view, and all the improvements
of the past five hundred years, you must admit,

53

resulted from my prompting. The labor movement?
Universal suffrage? The fundamental
belief in equal justice? They're all my doing,
and answers to the envy that first informed
those men and women that they were being treated
like beasts, like dirt. Why then does my name appear
on lists of prohibitions and taboos?
Precisely for that reason—that I disturb
the social order and make the nobles quake
in their huge dining rooms with the centerpieces
of silver and gold, the crystal chandeliers,
the flatware, the fine china, and all those footmen.
They count on it that wealth arouses envy
and hope that the peasants, believing what they've been told,
won't riot (at least not yet), for that would be sinful.

5 LUST

I have an affirmative defense. I am not only not
a sin but the subject of Jehovah's first commandment:
Be fruitful and multiply. How else does that happen,
do you suppose, and what demented church father
loathing the body, loathing himself, dreamed up
the perverse idea that lust was, in itself,
a bad thing? The Greeks, who were civilized—
at least for a while—thought of me as a god
and accorded me respect. What man or woman
can look at a painting or sculpture, never mind of a nude
but even a pot of flowers, a landscape, a still life,
without lust, or say an appreciation
of the sensuous forms the painter has on offer,
and not respond at all? I should not have been put here
on this ridiculous list, and whoever thinks
I deserve such a calumny ought to see
a shrink. People can, I concede, misuse
my gift, but that's their business. Love, children,
the survival of the species have their costs.

I invite you to take a walk with me in the springtime
when the girls first reappear in their summer dresses
and tell me it is not good to be alive.

6 GLUTTONY

What, I ask you, distinguishes me from hunger
that can't be a sin, except in the mind of some
self-abusing monk in his cell, despising
whatever is not pure spirit? Men are bodies,
and bodies need to be fed. But to answer the question,
gluttony is excess, some unattractive
fat rich man whom it's easy to laugh at.
There are, nevertheless, a few words
of explanation (not perhaps a defense
but at least an extenuation) for the deeper
question is the nature of his hunger
that he knows is unhealthy. His doctor, at every visit,
talks of his sleep apnea, his arthritis,
and his A1C hemoglobin that's high,
and the poor fellow would cut back if he could.
He resolves to do better, and tries, and fails.
That hunger of his isn't for food but for love.
He is sad, or beyond sad, and in his heartbreak
he needs to be consoled and he dimly remembers—
or cannot quite remember what his body
keeps, still, in its deepest recesses—lying
on his mother's breast, snug, warm, loved,
and being suckled, and he would give the world
to go back to that, but he can't, and instead he gorges,
stuffs himself, and never is satisfied.
But is that a moral defect? Or is it the world,
perilous and unfriendly as it is,
that deserves reproof? Show him a little compassion,
the understanding and love that he hungers for.

7 SLOTH

Not laziness, no, it's bigger than that. The older
name was better, *Accidie*, which suggests
a larger fatigue, not only of flesh but of spirit,
a failure, at last, of faith, and that indeed
would be a sin, that is if you believed
in sin. But my people don't. Perhaps they used to,
but now they get by on pills, the Lexapro
and maybe a little Wellbutrin. And their despair
may not indicate madness but sanity,
for they have seen through to the dismal truth of things—
that nothing lasts, that the dreams of their youth were merely
dreams. They grow up and age, and the body betrays,
and the mind, as it starts to consider the emptiness
that beckons, resigns itself. The childhood faith
they used to have seems quaint, or a bad joke.
There is no afterlife. There is no life.

TRANSLATIONS

"APRÈS LES VENTS, APRÈS LE TRISTE ORAGE" OF JEAN-ANTOINE DE BAÏF

After the winds, after the pitiless storms,
after a winter that flooded the oxen's furrows
turning them into rivers that crossed the farm's

bleak expanse, there's an end to the season's sorrows
as a gentler wind whispers its promise of spring
and yesterday's swamps dry out to make way for tomorrow's

fertile fields. But dear Lord, when will you bring
that gentle springtime to me? My tears still flow
in tempests as fierce as ever, and cold winds sting

of a bitter season still, for Love, with no
relenting that one would expect under such bright skies.
My inner landscape is one of pain and woe,

and the laughter of those around me I despise
as foolishness—or else an affront to me
and the endless tears that well up in my eyes.

In the woodland freshness that beckons, one can see
Venus and all her Graces celebrate
while their lovers dance before them gracefully.

Lewd mountain satyrs, too, participate,
trilling on oaten flutes their lively tunes
that delight the countryside and attract a mate

while, from the verdant glade, a nightingale croons—
Philomela mourning Itys? Or
merely birdsong? The pleasant afternoon's

blue sky brims with laughter; spirits soar;
and wood nymphs cavort alongside brooks that babble
in merriment that reminds me all the more

of the grief I feel. In misery and trouble,
my only songs are dirges and I feel
assaulted by all the happiness of this rabble

whose gaudy blues and greens cannot conceal
the universal blackness I know and trust:
the rosebud's hope is false; the canker is real.

These beauties of springtime to me are just
distractions from my mistress, whose frown and smile
determine my soul's weather. To you I must

refer, defer. In dead of winter, I'll
roast, or in summer shiver to your mood.
For me, spring flowers only blossom while

you suffer them to do so. The pretty wood
flourishes in your beauty that you grant
the world a share of because your heart is good.

Prettier than the spring itself, you want
to learn its gentleness, too. Your cruelty
must yield to mercy toward your postulant.

I yearn for that, and dream of an intimacy
at which you balk, as if you were terrified,
or do you merely test my loyalty
by your refusals, cold and unjustified?

"THE SIX ELEGIES OF SULPICIA"

I

At last, that love I wanted and have waited for has arrived,
      as I'm not ashamed to say. Why try to hide it?
My muse has interceded for me with the goddess of love,
      who granted my wish and brought him to me. Let Venus
enjoy this testimonial that she answers her suppliants' prayers,
      but I hesitate to let these words go forth
to anyone but him, who deserves to see them first.
      Lacking in maidenly modesty? What if I am?
I'm happy and even proud. Why should I be ashamed?
      Is he worthy of me? I'm the one who's done well.

II

My ridiculous birthday is here, and what is my big treat?
      A trip out to the country—without Cerinthus.
Where is the fun in that? Down on the farm it's cold
      and crude: no place for a girl. Uncle Messalla,
you mean well, but give me a break. If we go on that jaunt,
      I'll be leaving my mind—and heart—back here in Rome.
But what does what I want matter? Why do I even bother
      to want? You call the plays, you make the rules.

III

The birthday trip, I'm relieved to say, is off: your girl
      is allowed to spend her day, after all, in Rome—
with you, I hope. What a fine present this is. Good luck!
      And it turns out to be just what you'd wished for me.

IV

I've decided I am glad that you issued yourself that fun pass:
      otherwise, what a fool I'd have been, falling
into your arms. Go cavort with your slut and enjoy her

instead of Sulpicia, Servius' highborn daughter.
What would my family think if I were to condescend
    to be second fiddle to her, an utter nothing?

V

Do you worry yourself, Cerinthus, about your ailing girl
    and how this fever torments my exhausted body?
If you didn't wish me well, I shouldn't want to recover
    or have the will to fight this grievous illness.
What good would health be to me if you were undisturbed,
    and could think of me on this sickbed and not be troubled?

VI

May I never inflame your heart's passion, my love, as I did,
    it seems, a few days back: if in my life
I have ever misbehaved or done any foolish thing,
    I confess that I am even more ashamed
and regret more that I left you alone last night—in desire
    to conceal from you the desire that I was feeling.

"THE HERMIT AND THE MOUSE"
(from the *Hitopadesa*)

Deep in the woods in a humble hut,
a pious hermit lived, and what

should fall from the blue of the sky one day
but a mouse that a crow had snatched away

and then let drop? The hermit heard
its squeaks and he shooed the hungry bird

away. He cared for the mouse and tended
it back to health. When its hurts had mended,

the mouse became his pet and only
companion. (The hermit was pious but lonely.)

Some days later a cat came past
and frightened the mouse that ran as fast

as his little feet could take him back
to the hut where he would be safe from attack

by such large creatures with such sharp claws
and teeth. The kindly hermit, because

the mouse was his friend, cast a magic spell
that turned him into a dog that could well

defend himself from any bad
pussycats. And the mouse was glad,

delighted in fact. Then some days later
a tiger passed by, and the mouse felt greater

fear than ever before. He ran
as fast as he could to ask the man

who had helped him before to help again.
He cast another spell, and then

the dog became a tiger, too.
(There were no creatures, or very few,

he'd have had to worry about or fear.)
People and animals, far and near

told the amazing story of how
the hermit had changed his pet that now

appeared to be a tiger. "Appeared?"
The mouse would have preferred to be feared

by people and animals and even by
the hermit himself. The reason why

they didn't was that they thought of him yet
as a mouse, as the hermit's harmless pet.

The only way the mouse could see
to become that fearsome beast that he

believed he could be was to kill his friend,
the kindly hermit, and to that end

he crouched and prepared to pounce, but the master
could read his mind and prevented disaster

by turning the tiger poised to spring
to a mouse again, a harmless thing.

Had the mouse learned? With beady eyes
could it see the truth now? Had it grown wise?
Gratitude and loyalty are
stronger than tigers that terrorize.

"THE PHOENIX" OF LACTANTIUS

There is a happy place far off in the east where dawn
    first enters through the sky's eternal portals
to launch a new day on earth—between where the summer's glare
    commences and chill winter's wan sun rises.
This is the birthplace of balmy and delicate springtime mornings,
    and there, an inviting plain spreads out, a meadow
unmarred by any beetling hill or gaping chasm,
    and yet at such an altitude as to dwarf
our tallest mountain ridges by dozens of yards of height.
    This charming woodland, the grove of the Sun, is planted
with all manner of trees forever crowned in green.
    Even when Phaethon's car set the sky aflame,
this region remained unscathed; at the time of Deucalion's flood,
    no waves overwhelmed the verdure of these precincts.
Here Sickness dares not set foot, nor doddering Age,
    nor cruel Death, nor Fear, nor wicked Crime
approach, for Greed has not found this place, or murderous Rage.
    Grief is a stranger here, and Penury, too,
in its garb of woeful rags. The sleepless nights of Care
    are here unknown, and Hunger, abashed, hangs back.
The savage tempests never intrude, nor the howling winds
    resound, nor the painful fingers of frost prod
or harden the ground. In pellucid skies above no cloud
    stretches its fleecy blanket to darken the day;
no rain pours down, but a well in the heart of this blessed demesne,
    the well of life, gushes sweet crystal water
that flows forth in every season to irrigate and refresh
    the grateful grove. Here is the kind of tree
with a stately slender trunk that bears its mellow fruits
    that never fall to litter the ground below.
Here in this grove there lives the Phoenix, the nonpareil,
    the creature whose life is renewed by her own death,
an acolyte of Phoebus Apollo to whom she offers
    homage and serves as Nature herself commands.
As soon as Aurora reddens the sky with her rising, routing

the last of the laggard stars with her brighter light,
that bird plunges three times into the gentle water
to take three delicate sips from the living spring,
whereupon she soars again to perch on some lofty treetop
from which she can command the entire prospect,
and, turning to face to the east, she awaits the sun's fresh rising
to renew the day and the world with his radiant glory.
When the first of his bright beams have struck the heaven's portals,
she pours out her sweet notes of celebration,
summoning forth the morning in airs neither nightingale
nor any Cirrhean panpipe can ever equal.
Not even the dying swan can match her lyrical splendor,
and Mercury, listening, leaves his lyre untouched.
Once Phoebus has guided his steeds into the open
in their relentless course around the sky,
the bird appears to applaud, flapping her wings three times
and bowing her head thrice, and then she falls silent,
but accurately she marks the hours of day and night
as priestess of the wood and the god's faithful
acolyte, acquainted with the mysteries of time
and privileged to share Apollo's secrets.
When she approaches the end of her allotted span
of a thousand years and time has become a burden,
she flees her sweet and accustomed nest in that sacred grove
to seek this world in which Death holds dominion.
Old as she is, and weary, she makes haste for that Syria she
herself once named "Phoenice," where she finds
in its trackless wilderness a remote and hidden grove.
She chooses for herself a towering palm tree
with a crown that seems to reach to the heavens. That tree, named
for the bird that visits, "Phoenix," is sanctuary—
no harmful beast can come there, or slimy serpent ascend,
nor any bird of prey. Then Aeolus pens
the winds in their lofty caverns, lest any dare disturb
the clear air or drive dark clouds from the South
to obscure the light of the sun or endanger the delicate bird.
In that tree, she builds her nest, both grave and cradle,

for she dies in order to live, begetting a new self,
       and for this she gathers together from the woodlands
exotic spices and unguents, balms and fragrant herbs
       of the kind that wealthy Arabs collect, or Pygmies,
or Indian fakirs, or learned Egyptian mages who know
       the deep secrets of earth's abundant bosom.
She piles together cinnamon bark and the rich amomum
       that can waft for such great distance its pungent odor.
To these she adds the balsam, sweet cassia, tangy
       leaves of acanthus, drops of the rich oil
of frankincense, the hardy spikenard, and myrrh
       with its own special powers. Onto this nest,
this bestrewed life-giving couch, this catafalque, she arranges
       her body, and there with her beak anoints herself,
scattering over and under her limbs these preservative nostrums
       that constitute her rites of obsequy.
Surrounded by these perfumes she commends her soul to the god,
       trusting, fearless, and altogether faithful.
As her body catches the rays of the distant sun, it glows,
       and blazes into the flames of a life-giving death.
The fire at last subsides, reducing her to her ashes,
       which she compacts and fuses together to form
a mass that is a kind of seed from which there arises
       a limbless creature, a worm of milky color,
an imperfectly formed body that grows apace to the shape
       of a rounded egg with a shell, from which bursts forth—
as caterpillars we see in the fields that emerge from cocoons
       as butterflies—another miraculous phoenix,
what it was before but younger. She takes from this world no food
       not does any creature presume or attempt to feed her
while she remains unfledged, but she sips ambrosial dews
       that fall from the polestar, celestial nectars,
she thrives upon, and the nest's perfumed spices add
       mysterious powers. She reacquires her form,
color, and strength, and prepares to fly from her nest to return
       home. But first, she looks to her remains,
the bones of her former self and the ashes she mixes with myrrh

and frankincense, and with her mouth she rolls them
into a ball she grasps with her claws to bear aloft
    to the city of the sun, where, on the altar
she deposits it, a relic in the temple's sanctuary.
    There she presents herself for all to admire,
a creature of great beauty deserving of praise and honor,
    her color bright as the seeds of the pomegranate
that have ripened beneath the waxy rind or, say, as red
    as the poppy's scarlet blossoms when Flora has spread
her splendid cloak that seems to make even blue skies blush.
    The plumage of her shoulders and breast shines bright,
and there is a sheen to her neck and upper back that extends
    down to the brilliant tail, a metallic gold
with random purple markings as if it were bejeweled.
    Her wings are bright as any rainbow Iris
arranges across the sky to shame the mass of rain clouds.
    The beak is ivory white with emerald touches
that flash whenever she opens her mouth. Her eyes are large,
    of sapphire blue, but bright, lit from within.
And her head is crowned in the likeness of Apollo's own with a halo
    of radiating glory. Her legs are scaled
as if with golden greaves, and her claws are a rosy pink.
    Think of a pheasant, or, better, a proud peacock,
but even more grand, more gorgeous, and large as an African ostrich,
    that clumsy, camel-like bird that cannot fly
as the Phoenix can and does, with an easy grace and speed.
    Such is its manifestation before men's eyes,
and Egypt draws near to marvel at the wonder of its appearance
    and hail the peerless bird, the rara avis,
and salute and memorialize the great occasion, inscribing
    on the walls of their buildings the date of the apparition
and what it looked like to inform the generations to come
    what their good fortune had let them witness here.
Birds of every kind assemble to do her honor,
    putting aside for the moment their usual habits,
so that even raptors are tamed, and those they prey on are fearless,
    but, all united now in harmonious chorus,

they fly in attendance, soaring and wheeling in exultation
            to do the Phoenix honor and show their love.
Higher and higher, they rise in ever-widening circles
            until she surpasses them all in the loftiest regions
of that pure aether in which she feels herself at home,
            that blessed land to which she at last repairs.
O bird of destiny, happy creature, to whom the gods
            have given their singular gift—that she may beget
herself and may be thus reborn, neither male nor female,
            but both together, complete, needing no aid
from the flighty whims of Venus. Her god of love is Death,
            that constant, her pleasure, her sole and unfailing passion.
That she may be born again, she looks to Death as her gallant,
            and she is her own offspring, her own heir,
as she is her own nurse and her own delightful darling,
            herself and not herself, having transcended
mortality's logic, and constraints of life and time: from Death
            she has wrested the rare prize of eternal life.